JARROLD SHORT WALKS
leisure walks for all ages

Kent

Compiled by
Tony Durrant

JARROLD
publishing

Mapping
sourced from

Ordnance
Survey®

Acknowledgements

I would like to thank my wife, Katy, and son, Alfie, for being the guinea pigs for the shorter of these walks. Thanks also to Terry Marsh of the Outdoor Writers' Guild for his help and advice.

Text:	Tony Durrant
Photography:	Tony Durrant and Richard Watts
Editor:	Crawford Gillan
Designer:	Sarah Crouch

© Crimson Publishing, a division of Crimson Business Ltd

 This product includes mapping data licensed from Ordnance Survey® with the permission of the Controller of Her Majesty's Stationery Office.
© Crown Copyright 2002. All rights reserved. Licence number 100017593. Ordnance Survey, the OS symbol and Pathfinder are registered trademarks and Explorer, Landranger and Outdoor Leisure are trademarks of the Ordnance Survey, the national mapping agency of Great Britain.

ISBN 978-0-7117-2420-4

First published 2003 by Jarrold Publishing

This edition first published in Great Britain 2008 by Crimson Publishing, a division of:
Crimson Business Ltd
Westminster House, Kew Road
Richmond, Surrey, TW9 2ND
www.totalwalking.co.uk

Printed in Singapore
by Proost NV, Turnhout. 2/08

Front cover: Organic farmland on Henley Down
Previous page: Thatched cottage in Chillenden

Contents

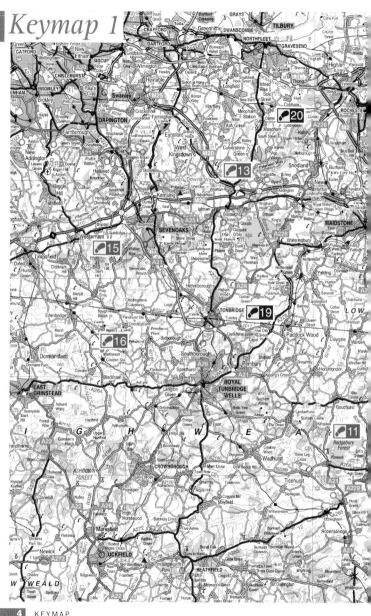

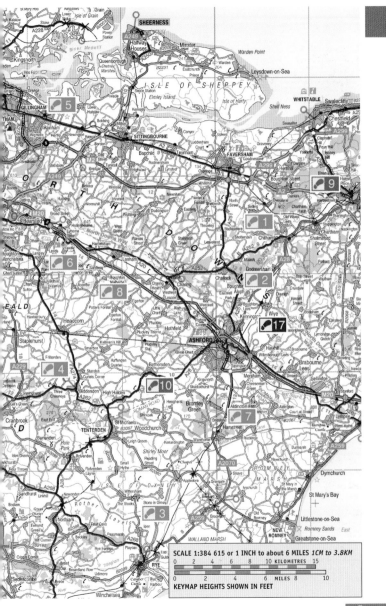

SCALE 1:384 615 or 1 INCH to about 6 MILES *1CM to 3.8KM*

0   2   4   6   8   10 KILOMETRES 15

0   2   4   6   MILES 8   10

KEYMAP HEIGHTS SHOWN IN FEET

Introduction

If there was ever a county designed for the country walker then Kent is it. The ancient routes that once linked so many rural communities have established themselves as a weblike network of rights of way, crossing and recrossing the landscape.

And what a landscape: coastline, rolling downs, chalk valleys, ancient woods, marshes and, of course, the rich fields, orchards and hop gardens that earned it the nickname of the Garden of England.

The county has many hidden villages that come complete with oak-beamed inns, ancient churches, thatched cottages and cricket pitches. This combination of tradition and scenery is why Kent is often regarded as the 'most English' of counties.

Gateway to an island

The first migrants to Kent travelled across the landbridge that linked Britain to Europe. Once the sea had forced the gap, the journey was made in boats by the Celts, Romans, Saxons, Jutes and Danes.

Christianity arrived in Kent in 597 with St Augustine landing at Ebbsfleet, starting the network of parishes that still exists today.

The county's proximity to Europe also put it in the front line in the event of war. For centuries, castles and ports guarded against invasion and when Napolean glowered across the Channel they were added to by another line of defence which included the Royal Military Canal.

Then Hitler threatened and, as the Battle of Britain raged in the Kentish skies, airfields and pillboxes sprang up around its fields and villages.

Long-distance paths

The little threads, myriad footpaths, bridleways, byways and narrow asphalt lanes used in this book, are linked by thicker strands, the long-distance routes.

Chief among them is the 141-mile (227km) North Downs Way which can be tramped from Farnham in Surrey in its long arc across Kent that ends with a flourish at the White Cliffs of Dover, those grand symbols of our island.

Then there is the Greensand Way, threading its 105 miles (168km) along a sandstone ridge from Haslemere in Surrey to finish at Hamstreet, just north of Romney Marsh.

Crossing the county from north to south is the 80-mile (128km) Wealdway, exploring the rolling hills and woodland of the Weald on its journey from Gravesend, on the River Thames, to Eastbourne on the Sussex coast. Hemming them all in is the Saxon Shore Way, the 140-mile (225km) coastal trail from Gravesend to Rye.

As our smaller routes draw small circles around the county, they often come across these bigger brothers in the way that old friends might bump into each other while out for a stroll.

People and places

Kent's position between the coast and London put it on the main trade route to Europe. The old inns we visit on these routes would have hummed with the latest news and gossip as merchant travellers to London and pilgrims to Canterbury passed this way.

This advantageous position also made Kent one of England's most prosperous areas. A place where rich merchants and London gentry built fine stately homes and mansions.

It was also a rebellious county, giving birth to two revolts against social inequality and misrule, and a thorn in the side of the law which was flouted by smugglers who used the coast in their own search for profit.

Thus, where Kent is concerned, there is no such thing as simply a walk in the country. A walk through Kent is a journey across a landscape filled with the echoes of people and historical upheaval as well as the obvious beauty of the physical and natural world.

1 *Perry Woods*

START Drawing Room car park

DISTANCE 1½ miles

TIME 1¼ hour

PARKING Drawing Room car park or Rose and Crown

ROUTE FEATURES A woodland walk on mud and shingle paths with two uphill climbs and one steep descent

This route explores coppiced woodland on undulating paths and bridleways that climb to reveal stunning views from the summit of the Mount and Windmill Hill. The history of the wood, preserved by Swale Borough Council, and its wildlife is well documented on signboards at the car park, known as the Drawing Room, and at the Rose and Crown, between the Mount and Windmill Hill.

✎ Leave the Drawing Room car park and cross the road to take the bridleway directly opposite, walking into mixed woodland with a coppiced area on the right. Follow the path uphill through rhododendrons. After rising to an area covered by a canopy of mature beech, drop to a plank bridge over a small stream before rising again.

? *What is a drey?*

🅐 Cross the driveway leading to Keepers Cottage and take the right fork, a bridleway, to climb a path criss-crossed by tree roots. Look upwards here for the dreys of squirrels.

At the top of the hill head directly south towards the Mount. The view opens out to the east, on the left, with few trees on the summit except silver birch pushing through a covering of bracken. Much of the mature woodland on this summit

PUBLIC TRANSPORT Trains to Selling from Canterbury. Enquiry line: 0845 7484950. Buses to Selling, Fridays only. Enquiry line: 0870 6082608

REFRESHMENTS Rose and Crown with outside tables, or Badgers Hill, at junction of New Cut Road and A252, a petting farm with teashop, open 9am–5pm, Monday–Friday

PUBLIC TOILETS None

ORDNANCE SURVEY MAP Explorer 149 (Sittingbourne & Isle of Sheppey)

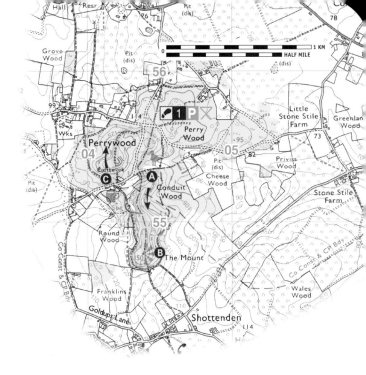

was blown down by the 1987 hurricane. The view to the west is the next attraction before the path passes a stand of Scots pine to reach the wooden viewing platform called the Pulpit.

B There are benches and picnic tables beneath the Pulpit, making it an ideal spot to take in the lovely views of rolling fields and orchards. On leaving the Pulpit, carry on in a southerly direction to descend by a steep stepped path. This meets the bridleway going around the base of the Mount.

Coppicing in Perry Woods

Views from the Mount

Turn right here rather than crossing the stile and follow the bridleway as it turns towards the north with the wooded slopes of the Mount on the right. Ignore paths off to the left and right, but wait until the path meets a driveway of a house. Turn left and take the driveway, a track, as it descends gently, passing the car park and garden of the Rose and Crown, a 16th-century pub.

The wooden structure, or Pulpit, on the **Mount** was built on the spot once occupied by another structure believed to be one of the Royal Navy signalling stations that linked the Kent coast to the Admiralty in London before the invention of telephone and radio communications.

C Take the bridleway by the gritting bin near the front of the Rose and Crown. It climbs steeply up Windmill Hill, which also has picnic tables at its summit. Pass lots of Scots pine on the left then the right. At one point the land drops away steeply to the right of the path where there is an area of banks and dips used by mountain bikers. There is a pine needle carpet underfoot now as the path descends. Go straight ahead where paths join on the right, then bear left to descend to an asphalt track by a gate and a Swale Borough Council sign. Turn left on the road for a few yards then right at the crossroads to return to the entrance to the Drawing Room car park.

Foxgloves in Perry Woods

King's Wood

START King's Wood car park and picnic area
DISTANCE 1.5 miles
TIME 1¼ hours
PARKING Free at King's Wood picnic site and car park

2

The ancient forest of King's Wood was named after King John who hunted there in the 12th century. The fallow deer that still live in the wood, owned by the Forestry Commission, are now protected and have been joined by some larger animals and insects, commissioned by the Stour Valley Art Project. They will delight the young.

From the car park follow the sign for picnic site, walks and sculpture. Various kinds of wood sculpture, mainly animals and insects, are soon seen among the grass and trees. Pass the information panel on the Stour Valley Art Project just before the path comes into a large coppiced clearing.

There is a three-mile route marked by wooden posts with white bootprints. This route follows some of that walk. Take the obvious path that descends along the left side of the clearing and follow it into the wood.

A Cross a forestry track, ignoring the Short Cut sign, and carry on into the wood, following the post with the white bootprint. Watch for a large sculpture on the left among an area of more mature trees. This area is used by youth

ROUTE FEATURES Easy paths through mixed woodland with no steep climbs or descents
PUBLIC TRANSPORT Trains to Wye from Ashford and Canterbury. Enquiry line: 0845 7484950. Buses to Challock from Canterbury. Enquiry line: 0870 6082608
REFRESHMENTS Halfway House, Challock, has a play area. Tickled Trout, Wye, has a large garden
PUBLIC TOILETS None
ORDNANCE SURVEY MAP Explorer 137 (Ashford, Headcorn, Chilham & Wye)

groups and is sometimes dotted with makeshift shelters. At the next forest track that crosses the path, do not follow the white bootprint marker. Turn right along the track as it descends for 100 yds (92m) to meet another track at a crossroads in a shallow valley.

B Turn right here and climb gently with mainly coniferous trees on the left for 250 yds (230m) to meet another track. Go straight across this, following the sign for the car park. Now and again there

Easy well-marked paths

Look for the woodland shelters

are narrow paths going off this main path leading into small clearings that are ideal for children to explore. Watch for the three huge woven wood sculptures on the right. The path rises to a junction signed with the white bootprint. Go to the right through dense woodland. Ignore the path to the left by the old yew.

Continue until the path emerges at the clearing you passed on the outward leg. Turn left and pass more sculptures to return to the car park and the starting point of the walk.

? *What is the name of the poisonous snake that lives in King's Wood?*

One of many wood sculptures

3 # The Isle of Oxney and the Royal Military Canal

START Crown Inn

DISTANCE 1½ miles

TIME 1¼ hours

PARKING Free on The Street or in layby on Church Hill, opposite church

This route starts in the hamlet of Stone in Oxney on the higher ground of the Isle of Oxney and descends across farmland to easy walking along the Royal Military Canal before climbing moderately to return to the village

Turn right out of the Crown Inn, following the sign for the Saxon Shore Way, into The Street, passing the parish council noticeboard and the memorial hall. Turn right after 250 yds (230m) onto the driveway of a house and head for the gate into a field. The church can be seen on the left across the field. Do not head towards the church but continue forward along the edge of the field to a stile by a metal gate. Do not cross this stile.

? *Why was the Royal Military Canal built?*

A Turn left, taking the footpath towards the church, crossing a small stream in a dip. Enter the churchyard of St Mary the Virgin through a gate beneath a horse chestnut tree. Leave the churchyard by the stepped path leading onto the asphalt road, called Church Hill, and turn left to cross a stile by a National Trust sign. Veer towards the right to cross this field to another stile in a small stretch of wooden fencing. Head across this field, bearing slightly left, by descending towards the left edge of some trees in a shallow valley. Cross the stile and

ROUTE FEATURES Grassy paths across farmland descending to a canal. Moderate uphill route on return leg

PUBLIC TRANSPORT Buses from Tenterden. Enquiry line: 0870 6082608

REFRESHMENTS Crown Inn, outside tables

PUBLIC TOILETS None

ORDNANCE SURVEY MAP Explorer 125 (Romney Marsh, Rye & Winchelsea)

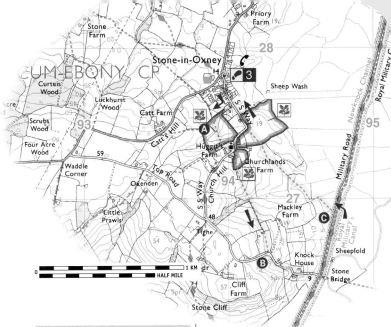

Oxney is called an island because travel to it from all directions involves using a bridge to cross water.

the stream and head upwards along the edge of the field to a stile by a metal gate. Take this and continue through a series of paddocks using stiles, keeping Mackley Farm to the left, to meet the asphalt lane by the driveway to Mackley Farm.

B Turn left along the lane and descend, via twists and turns, towards the Royal Military Canal. Cross the drainage dyke by a bridge then cross the Military Road to turn left onto the Royal Military Canal path.

Parish sign for Stone and Ebony

Follow this path, also the Saxon Shore Way, along the embankment for 500 yds (460m). Take the stile through the hedge and turn right along the road for 50 yds (46m) to the footbridge across the dyke on the left.

The Royal Military Canal

C Head diagonally right across the field (in the direction of the church tower on the horizon) to a wooden footpath marker post. Turn left from this marker to a stile by a metal fence. Take the stile and head diagonally across the field to the opposite corner, crossing a plank bridge over a dyke. Take the stile into a large field and turn right to cross it, towards a stile by a metal gate far to the right of a large barn. Cross this stile and aim for

the telegraph pole where there is a ladder stile in the hedge leading onto the bend in Church Hill. Turn right to return to the village or left towards the church.

> A **Roman altarstone** thought to be dedicated to the god Mithras was discovered here and stands in the church tower. A bull can still be seen carved into one side of it.

Stone village from St Mary the Virgin

Sissinghurst Castle

START Sissinghurst Castle car park
DISTANCE 2 miles
TIME 1½ hours
PARKING Free at Sissinghurst Castle car park
ROUTE FEATURES Flat paths and tracks around castle grounds and nearby farmland

This route starts at Sissinghurst Castle and explores the farmland surrounding it. The National Trust-owned estate, a jewel in the crown of the Weald, offers well-kept gardens and other attractions. Visitors should note that the shop, restaurant and gardens will be closed on Wednesdays and Thursdays in 2003 but the car park will be open.

From the car park follow signs for the castle, passing the public toilets, oast-house exhibition and Granary restaurant to take the path between the main house and the National Trust shop. The track runs by the moat, giving views of the tower and glimpses of the gardens.

A At the corner of the moat the public right of way, a bridleway, runs straight ahead between fields (*For smaller walks around the*

Sissinghurst Castle is not a castle in the medieval sense but more like a manor house. It was called a castle by French prisoners of war from 1756 to 1763 and the name stuck.

estate lakes and Roundshill Park Wood turn right here). Follow the bridleway by a hedge as it heads towards a line of trees in the distance. Cross Hammer Stream by a bridge to rise gently towards a copse on the horizon and a gate onto an asphalt lane.

PUBLIC TRANSPORT Buses from Staplehurst and Maidstone. Enquiry line: 0870 6082608. Trains to Staplehurst from Tonbridge or Ashford Enquiry line: 0845 7484950
REFRESHMENTS Granary restaurant
PUBLIC TOILETS Sissinghurst Castle
ORDNANCE SURVEY MAP Explorer 137 (Ashford, Headcorn, Chilham & Wye)

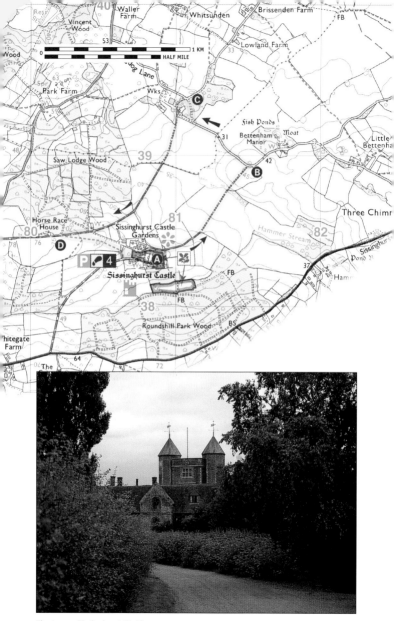

The tower, Sissinghurst Castle

Farmland near Sissinghurst Castle

B Turn left here. The lane descends gently, crossing a stream to give views of the castle to the left. Follow the lane as it curves right to enter a wood. Leave the lane at a T-junction.

C Turn left along the bridleway which runs up the left-hand of two driveways to pass the front of a house. Enter a field and carry on with the trees on the right, ignoring double gates on the right. Continue ahead as the path becomes a tunnel between high hedges and trees. Cross farm tracks going into fields on the right as more views of the castle appear on the left. Do not turn left at a house but walk past it to take the left path by the wooden gate at the corner of

Who created the gardens at Sissinghurst?

the wood. After 250 yds (230m) take the stile in the hedgerow on the left by the telegraph pole and leave the wood.

D Bear diagonally left across the field towards a stile in a hedge then bear right across a grassy area used for overflow parking at the castle. Walk by a picnic area, screened by trees, to a gap in a hedge and a footpath marker. Follow these markers through more hedges to return to the main car park. ●

Admission to the **castle** gardens is by ticket only on a timed basis to reduce overcrowding.

5 Riverside Country Park

This linear walk begins from the car park at the Riverside Country Park. Information boards and the visitor centre provide much detail about the park and its wildlife. The route follows the Saxon Shore Way along the coast and is never far from the mudflats and water of the Medway Estuary. Return by the same route.

START Riverside Country Park car park

DISTANCE 2½ miles

TIME 1½ hours

PARKING Free at Riverside Country Park car park

ROUTE FEATURES Flat path and track that is popular with cyclists. No stiles. Children's playground at Riverside Country Park

From the car park walk straight to the water's edge to pick up the Saxon Shore Way. Turn right onto this path from where the causeway leading to Horrid Hill can be seen. Follow the Saxon Shore Way through coastal grassland and scrub close to the mudflats and reedbeds. It is these environments that make the park an attractive habitat to birds and insects. Watch for avocet, dunlin, common tern and shelduck as well as butterflies such as the small tortoiseshell, peacock and the painted lady.

The area has been used for industry since the Romans manufactured salt and pottery here. **Horrid Hill**, which was formerly an island, had a causeway built to it about 100 years ago to carry a horse-drawn railway that took locally-quarried chalk to a cement factory.

Ⓐ The byway to the right, before the start of Bloors Wharf, leads to the Three Mariners pub at Lower

PUBLIC TRANSPORT Trains from Chatham and Sittingbourne to Rainham. Enquiry line: 0845 7484950
Buses from Chatham. Enquiry line: 0870 6082608
REFRESHMENTS Café and tables at Riverside Country Park. The Three Mariners pub has a garden
PUBLIC TOILETS Riverside Country Park
ORDNANCE SURVEY MAP Explorer 148 (Maidstone & the Medway Towns) or Explorer 163 (Gravesend & Rochester)

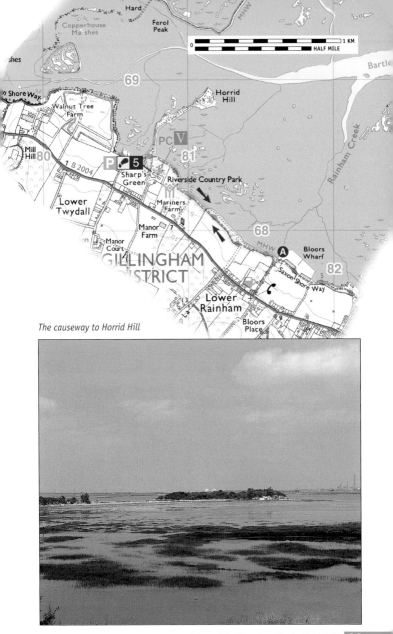

The causeway to Horrid Hill

The Saxon Shore Way follows the Kent coastline

The **Saxon Shore Way** is a long-distance footpath that follows the coastline of Kent from Gravesend to Rye, just over the East Sussex border. In places, it follows the line of defences that the Romans built around the coast to repel Saxon raiders.

How many people does Riverside Country Park attract each year?

Rye. To return to the country park retrace the outward route.

Rainham, a handy diversion for lunch. The wharf was originally used by fishermen to put to sea. Follow the Saxon Shore Way past the wharf, taking the right-hand path when it branches, to a small car park. From here the Saxon Shore Way continues its 140-mile journey round the Kent coast to

The **Medway Estuary** is protected as part of the Medway Marches Site of Special Scientific Interest (SSSI). A SSSI is any land which is deemed to be important because of its flora, fauna, geological or physiographical features. The Medway Estuary is particularly important as it is the home to large numbers of wintering birds which feed on the mudflats.

Leeds and its castle

Starting at the church of St Nicholas, in the village of Leeds, the path crosses fields onto the Leeds estate to run beside a lake by the castle then along a minor road through the village of Broomfield. The return journey is through mixed woods and fields.

START The church of St Nicholas in Leeds
DISTANCE 2½ miles
TIME 2 hours
PARKING Free in Wykeham Grove by the George inn, Leeds
ROUTE FEATURES Gentle walking over the Leeds Castle estate and surrounding farmland. Short stretch on a minor road

6

A Saxon church was built on the site of **St Nicholas' Church** in 1000. In 1200, the Normans added the tower. The tower houses ten bells, including one weighing one ton which was cast in 1617.

Start the walk at the church of St Nicholas at the northern end of the village of Leeds. Walk through the graveyard and keep straight on.

A Cross the road and carry on, along the edge of a cricket field to a gate. Two paths lead from here. Take the path towards Leeds Castle and fine views can be glimpsed

The route gives superb views of the castle

PUBLIC TRANSPORT Trains from Maidstone and Ashford to Eyhorne Street. Enquiry line: 0845 7484950. Buses from Maidstone to Leeds. Enquiry line: 0870 6082608
REFRESHMENTS George Inn with a beer garden and the Ten Bells, both in Leeds
PUBLIC TOILETS None
ORDNANCE SURVEY MAP Explorer 148 (Maidstone & the Medway Towns)

What do the Ten Bells
pub in Leeds and the
church of St Nicholas
have in common?

along this path. As the lake, the
Great Water, is approached bear
right after the car park entrance to
cross a stile and walk close to the
water's edge. At the end of the lake
cross another stile and walk over a
bridge. Take the path to the road
and turn right, passing through the
village of Broomfield. Pass the
church on the left and after 130 yds
(120m) turn right.

Leeds Castle and the Great Water

Leeds Castle, called the
loveliest castle in the world,
was started nearly 900 years ago. It
has been home to six English queens
and numerous royal and important
persons have passed through the
gates.

B Follow the path as it enters the
garden of a house then leaves it
through trees. After 100 yds (92m)
bear right and skirt woodland
before entering it. On the other
side, look out for a fine view of the
castle. Cross an estate road and
pass the cricket field to rejoin the
original path back to St Nicholas'
Church.

Hamstreet Woods

7

START Car park by Hamstreet playing fields

DISTANCE 2½ miles

TIME 2 hours

PARKING Free car park by Hamstreet playing fields

ROUTE FEATURES Flat paths and tracks through mixed wooodland.

This route explores the English Nature reserve at Hamstreet Woods, renowned for its wide variety of moths and butterflies. It then crosses farmland to give extensive views over Romney Marsh before returning through the woods.

From the car park turn left along the road, passing the post office and School House restaurant, to turn right at the Duke's Head into Duke's Meadow. Turn left by the pillbox following a sign for the Saxon Shore Way to leave the village along an asphalt lane. At the end of the lane, turn right into Hamstreet Woods nature reserve.

A Cross a bridge and take the left path to follow the Saxon Shore Way past the English Nature information panel. After 150 yds (138m) turn right where the path

Hamstreet Woods are home to a variety of moths such as merveille-du-jour and the light orange underwing. Watch and listen for nightingales in the spring, tawny owls in autumn evenings and bush crickets and glow-worms in the summer.

forks to stay on the Saxon Shore Way. As the path becomes a wide grassy ride ignore paths and tracks going off left and right. The track curves right to a small gate by a five-bar gate. Go through this and after 250 yds (230m) leave the Saxon Shore Way to turn right on a byway.

PUBLIC TRANSPORT Trains to Hamstreet from Hastings and Ashford. Enquiry line: 0845 7484950
Buses to Hamstreet from Ashford. Enquiry line: 0870 6082608

REFRESHMENTS The Schoolhouse restaurant and Duke's Head both have outside tables

PUBLIC TOILETS None

ORDNANCE SURVEY MAP Explorer 125 (Romney Marsh, Rye & Winchelsea, Tenterden & New Romney)

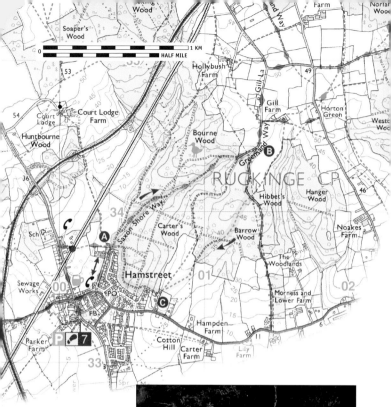

B The byway leads through a tunnel of trees. Ignore a gate on the right after 300 yds (276m) but watch for a stile 75 yds (69m) farther on. Cross the stile and return to the wood.

Leaving Hamstreet Woods

The path descends, crossing another path. Ignore a path to the right running through a coppiced area where brambles thrive on the woodland floor. At a stile in a gate, where there are views across Romney Marsh, leave the woodland and strike out across a

Romney Marsh and the Channel from the woods

field, aiming for a metal gate in the trees on the horizon to the right of Hampden Farm.

C Walk towards a driveway and turn right, before a garage, to the stile. Take the left of two paths leading downhill into the trees, curving as it runs parallel with the edge of the woods. Turn left at a T-junction of paths and head downhill to emerge by the information panel at the start of the walk. ●

Why were pillboxes built?

Following the path across farmland

8 *Egerton and the Greensand Way*

This route starts at Egerton, a scenic village with a vibrant rural community, and follows the Greensand Way through orchards and woodland to the edge of Coldbridge Wood where it follows an old byway before returning through farmland.

DISTANCE 2½ miles
TIME 2 hours
PARKING Free at Egerton village hall
ROUTE FEATURES Easy paths and tracks with some careful route-finding and stile-spotting needed in places where paths across fields are not obvious. Children's play area at Egerton village hall

In 1942 farmland to the south west of **Egerton** had its hedgerows ripped out and fields flattened to create an airfield for Spitfires of the RAF. Wing Commander Johnny Johnson, the RAF's highest scoring fighter ace of the Second World War was stationed here.

Leave the car park to turn right up Rock Hill Road, passing the George Inn. Join the Greensand Way by turning left into the churchyard of St James' Church. Leave the graveyard through a gate into an orchard and take the path that cuts through the orchard, angling slowly away from

Following the Greensand Way

PUBLIC TRANSPORT Buses from Ashford. Enquiry line: 0870 6082608
REFRESHMENTS The George Inn has outside tables and tearooms
PUBLIC TOILETS None
ORDNANCE SURVEY MAP Explorer 137 (Ashford, Headcorn, Chilham & Wye)

An old timber and tile farmhouse by the path

the mature trees on the left. Pass a copse of mixed woodland, go through a five-bar gate and follow the Greensand Way along a grassy avenue to a gate by two stiles. Pass Egerton House to meet Egerton House Road.

Ⓐ Cross the road to the stile from which two footpaths start. Take the one on the right which leads gently downwards towards woodland by the edge of the field. Take a stile into the trees and a stepped path that leads into a field surrounded by trees. Walk straight across the field towards a track into another field. From here watch for the directions of the arrows on the stiles and gates as the Greensand Way threads its way across small fields surrounded by trees to cross two plank bridges then skirt fields where Wellham Wood and the higher rise of the Greensand ridge lie on the right.

Take a plank bridge across a ditch to where the Greensand Way meets a byway by the edge of Coldbridge Wood.

Ⓑ Leave the Greensand Way here and turn left along the byway with

Looking across the Weald from the Greensand Ridge

Coldbridge Wood on the right. The path is lined by hedges and trees until it ends at a metal gate with a stile into a field. Skirt this field to the left, heading towards two gates in the corner.

C Take the left-hand gate and the path towards a large lone oak. After the oak, carry on across the field (leaving the byway which goes through a gate on the right). Aim for the stile by the gate in the hedge near the left-hand of two houses at the far side of the field. The house, Star and Garter Cottage, is on Egerton House

Road. Cross the road and go straight ahead to follow the hedge as it turns left then right, rising gently. Cross a stile on the left and turn immediately right to come out onto a lane by a house.

D Turn left along the lane for 30 yds (28m), and where the road curves left, head up a path by a beech hedge towards Lark Hill, passing a black and white timbered house. Take wooden steps into a field and turn right along a fence. Leave the fence at its corner and head across the field towards the tower of St James' Church in

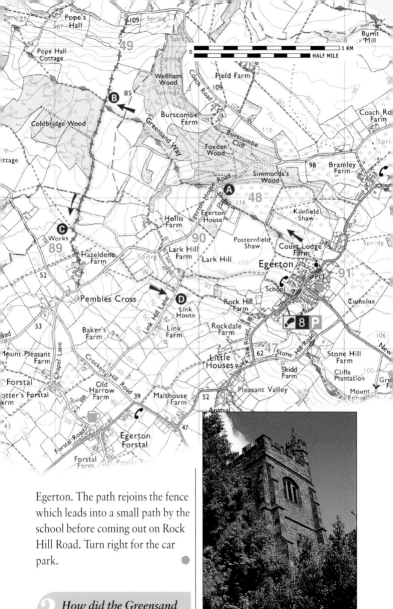

Egerton. The path rejoins the fence which leads into a small path by the school before coming out on Rock Hill Road. Turn right for the car park.

? *How did the Greensand Way get its name?*

Take the path past St James' Church

9

Blean Woods and Upper Harbledown

START Blean Woods
DISTANCE 2½ miles
TIME 2 hours
PARKING Free at the RSPB car park in Blean Woods
ROUTE FEATURES Forest trails, some muddy paths, occasional stiles, some ascent and descent, particularly leaving Upper Harbledown

From the RSPB reserve at Blean Woods this route explores both mature and coppiced woodland by forest tracks and paths. It descends by a stream to the village of Upper Harbledown before returning through the woods on a well-signed bridleway via the outskirts of Rough Common.

See the information panel at the RSPB car park in Blean Woods and the forest sculpture before setting off. Although the RSPB have provided a selection of their own signed walks this one follows public rights-of-way inside and outside the reserve. Turn right out of the car park along the forest track and follow it for about 900 yds (828m), passing through mixed woodland of mainly oak and beech. Ignore two rutted tracks going off to the left and watch for a path crossing the track where there is a post with a dog-walking symbol.

A Turn left and follow the path, rutted and muddy in parts, through coppiced woodland. In summer, watch for the heath fritillary butterfly, also called the woodsman's follower because it lives on the exposed land in the coppiced areas. Turn right at a path T-junction and after about 100 yds (92m) watch for wooden posts pointing out a path going off to

What is the purpose of the building on the Upper Harbledown village sign?

PUBLIC TRANSPORT Buses to Rough Common from Canterbury. Enquiry line: 0870 6082608
REFRESHMENTS Shops and bar meals at Dog and Bear pub, Rough Common. Bar meals and garden at the Plough, Upper Harbledown
PUBLIC TOILETS None
ORDNANCE SURVEY MAP Explorer 150 (Canterbury & the Isle of Thanet)

the left. Take this narrower path into denser woodland. This path dog-legs through the trees then gently descends with a stream in a deep gully to a two-plank bridge across the stream. Cross and climb with the stream on the left to emerge from the wood behind St Mary's Hall.

B Turn left here and follow the footpath into Upper Harbledown, passing the ornate village sign. Pass the Plough and the entrance to Harbledown Lodge and ignore the stile and footpath sign shortly after

Result of coppicing in Blean Woods

Welcome to Upper Harbledown

descends to cross two streams then rises as it heads towards Rough Common. Houses are soon seen through the trees and an asphalt path is underfoot.

D Pass the houses and after 25 yds (23m) turn left on the footpath sign after house number 17. Cross the end of a cul-de-sac to take the path between houses 12 and 13. The path passes back gardens to come out onto the forest track. Turn left to return to the car park. ●

it. Instead, watch for the bridleway on the left just as the road curves to the right.

C Take the bridleway that rises steadily then levels, allowing comfortable walking through trees. Follow the bridleway markers as the path widens into a track, passing coppiced woodland on the right. Follow the bridleway as it

It is unusual to find such large expanses of unspoiled woodland in the South East of England and the RSPB jumped at the chance to buy **Blean Woods** in 1981. The car park is open 8am to 9pm while access on foot is allowed outside of these times for those who, at the right time of year, want to listen to nightingales and nightjars.

The routes through the woods are well signed

Bethersden and Twenty Acre Wood

This route starts from Bethersden, by the children's play area, and explores picturesque hay meadows and woodland to the south of the village.

START Car park by Bethersden tennis club
DISTANCE 2½ miles
TIME 2 hours
PARKING Free by Bethersden Tennis Club
ROUTE FEATURES A flat walk across farmfields and meadows on little-used paths.Children's play area by tennis courts, near car park

Leave the car park and turn left along Mill Road to the junction by the memorial to King George. Turn left along Forge Hill, passing oast-houses and the village hall, to the junction with the A28.

Ⓐ Turn left for 30 yds (28m) then turn right to take the stile onto the footpath between gardens. Take the stiles across small fields to come out by a small market garden. From here, bear left across the field to a stile by a gate in the hedgerow. Cross the stile and turn right to follow the hedgerow. Cross the stream by a plank bridge with a stile in a gate. Continue straight ahead up the meadow, following

Village memorial to King George

PUBLIC TRANSPORT Buses from Ashford. Enquiry line: 0870 6082608
REFRESHMENTS Shops and the George pub, Bethersden, with garden and play area
PUBLIC TOILETS None
ORDNANCE SURVEY MAP Explorer 137 (Ashford, Headcorn, Chilham & Wye)

Pond among the hay meadows

C Stay in the field and turn hard right to take the path along the edge of the field, passing ponds in the wood to the left. Leave the field by a gate and continue straight ahead to another gate into the wood. Do not take the track curving left out of the wood but walk straight ahead to pick up the path through the trees. Leave the wood at a stile in the corner of a meadow. Follow the edge of the meadow to a stile on the left and a footbridge over a stream.

the line of the telegraph poles, towards the trees of Twenty Acre Wood. As the field narrows, bear left and watch for the first of two stiles.

B Take the stile into the wood. After 75 yds (69m) leave the wood by a stile. Cross the field by bearing slightly left towards a metal field gate and the stile hidden in the hedgerow 10 yds (9m) beyond it. Do not cross this stile but turn to the right, passing to the left of a large pond, towards two metal gates in the corner of the field. Take the stile by the left gate into another field. Cross this field, bearing right, to the diagonally opposite corner. Do not cross the stile in the corner of the field.

D Cross the bridge and bear diagonally right across a field towards the hedge to the left of some ponds. Take the stile into a field with Low Wood Farm at the far side. Follow the edge of the field and, after 150 yds (138m), watch for the lone horse chestnut tree at the point where the fence changes direction. By it, is a partially hidden stile. Take the stile and cross the field, taking the right of two paths, heading to the right of a pond towards a kissing gate by the pavilion of Bethersden Cricket Club.

? *What year was Bethersden Cricket Club founded?*

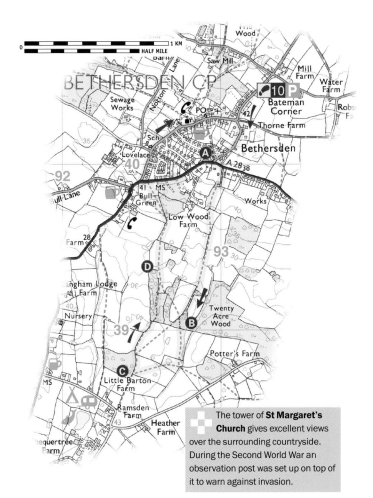

BETHERSDEN CP

Bethersden

The tower of **St Margaret's Church** gives excellent views over the surrounding countryside. During the Second World War an observation post was set up on top of it to warn against invasion.

Cross the cricket field to a gate and turn left along the A28 to the junction with School Road. Turn right, pass the school and head for St Margaret's Church and the George pub. Pass the George to return to the outward leg at the junction with Mill Road.

St Margaret's Church, Bethersden

11 *Bedgebury Forest*

START Bedgebury Pinetum car park

DISTANCE 3 miles

TIME 2½ hours

PARKING Free at Bedgebury Pinetum car park

ROUTE FEATURES The pinetum is set in undulating, landscaped gardens with good paths, while the nature trail is flat and passes through a range of forest habitats

Bedgebury National Pinetum contains the finest collection of conifers in the world. There are many routes through the forest, taking in more than 6,000 trees in landscaped gardens and lakes. This walk explores the pinetum and landscaped gardens before taking in a nature trail with many information points.

Take the path through the entrance gate of the pinetum which leads onto a lovely view of the landscaped gardens and lakes.

A A number of walks start here. This route follows the circular walk along the asphalt path to the right. The path drops down and then rises. Look out for conifer-loving birds, such as hawfinches, firecrests and crossbills.

Continue along the path to the toilets at the far side of the pinetum. Pass the toilets, cross the road and go through the gate to pick up the forest nature trail.

B The nature trail passes a number of experimental forest plots with information signs. The

The **pinetum** was founded by the Forestry Commission and the Botanic Gardens at Kew. It was originally designed by William Dallimore and the first trees were planted in 1925. Many of the oldest and largest examples of conifers in Britain grow here, as well as rare, endangered and historically important trees.

PUBLIC TRANSPORT Buses from Royal Tunbridge Wells to Kilndown. Enquiry line: 0870 6082608

REFRESHMENTS Coffee shop at the pinetum

PUBLIC TOILETS In the Pinetum

ORDNANCE SURVEY MAP Explorer 136 (The Weald, Royal Tunbridge Wells, Cranbrook, Hawkhurst & Bewl Water)

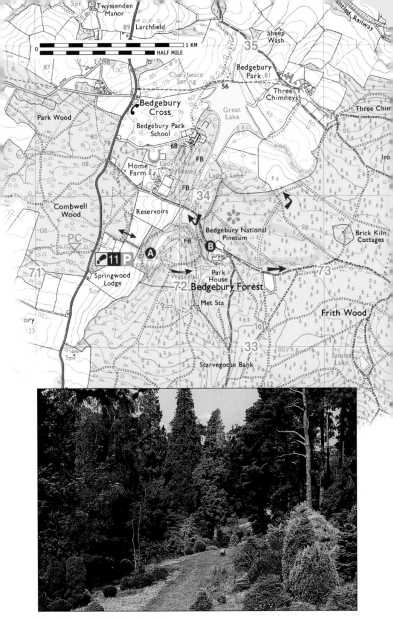

The pinetum at Bedgebury Forest

route is clearly marked by white arrows around the grass footpaths and tracks. Follow the arrows back to the start of the nature trail. Recross the road and turn right by the toilets to continue through the main part of the pinetum. Take the bridge over the end of the large lake which has a thriving duck population. This is a good place for a picnic and there are tables on the grass. Follow the path past another smaller lake and climb to the original viewing point near the entrance. ●

Easy walking through the nature trail

? *The tallest tree in Kent is growing in the pinetum. What is its name?*

Open views of the pinetum

Goodnestone and Chillenden

START Car park by Goodnestone House

DISTANCE 3.5 miles

TIME 3 hours

PARKING Free by Goodnestone House

ROUTE FEATURES Easy paths and tracks with no steep ground

This route joins two picture postcard villages by easy paths. It starts at Goodnestone Park gardens and its 30-year-old stately home which are open to the public in the summer. Jane Austen was a frequent visitor.

From the entrance to the gardens take the track by the cricket field towards the timbered buildings of Bonnington Farm. Turn left at the asphalt lane by the farm, noting the arched windows on some of the buildings. This design is said to bring good luck. Pass the pond and carry on past the T-junction to leave the lane where it bends sharply left.

Ⓐ Two footpaths leave this point. Take the left one through the field towards the edge of the trees on the horizon. Pass to the left of the line of trees and carry on with the trees of Nooketts Wood across the fields to the left. At the corner of the playing fields take the stile and turn left for 200 yds (184m) to leave by a gate. Turn right out of the gate, ignoring the gap in the trees on the right, to head along the edge of the treeline. Pass the garden gate of a house which has 1867 inscribed on its wall, and follow its drive to the byway, Cherrygarden Lane.

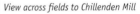
View across fields to Chillenden Mill

PUBLIC TRANSPORT Buses from Canterbury. Enquiry line: 0870 6082608

REFRESHMENTS Tearoom at Goodnestone gardens from Mar to Oct; FitzWalter Arms and Griffin's Head serve food and have gardens

PUBLIC TOILETS Outside at the Griffin's Head

ORDNANCE SURVEY MAP Explorer 150 (Canterbury & the Isle of Thanet)

B Turn right to descend gently down the byway. Chillenden village can be seen across to the left. Pass Gooseberry Hall Farm and turn left at the corner of the paddock by the metal gate. Follow the path towards Chillenden behind which the white sails of Chillenden Mill can be seen. When the road is reached turn right for

Timbered buildings at Bonnington Farm

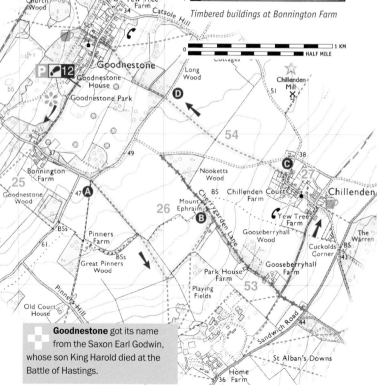

Goodnestone got its name from the Saxon Earl Godwin, whose son King Harold died at the Battle of Hastings.

the Griffin's Head pub or left to continue the route towards All Saints' Church. Pass the church and follow the lane round to the right.

C Turn left by the thatched cottage and follow the path across a field to steps down to a lane. Cross the lane and climb to a stile into a field with a view of the windmill. Cross the field towards the lone tree on the horizon and the stile beneath it. Cross another field to the road by Long Wood.

D Take the stile into the wood and cross a track eventually to head diagonally right towards some modern houses on the edge of Goodnestone. Turn left in a paddock and take a cement drive to The Street. Turn left to pass the FitzWilliam Arms and return to the car park. ●

Chillenden Mill

Chillenden Mill is open to the public on bank holidays and Sundays, May to September, 2pm–4.30pm.

What year is inscribed on the wall of Forge Cottage?

Village cricket at Goodnestone

13 *Great Wood and an ancient grave*

From Trosley Country Park this route offers easy walking through Great Wood, on the North Downs, then descends to explore the ancient burial site of Coldrum Long Barrow before following in the footsteps of countless Canterbury pilgrims who have called at the ancient church in the hamlet of Trosley Court. There is a steep final section to regain the crest of the downs.

START Trosley Country Park

DISTANCE 3½ miles

TIME 3 hours

PARKING Honesty box, 8.30am to 7.30pm, in the country park

ROUTE FEATURES Easy tracks through woods at the beginning, then easy paths across farmland and chalk downland. There is one steep section at the end.

Go south out of the car park at the country park by the large information board and descend to two more information panels on the North Downs Way. Turn left here and head east, ignoring paths to the left and right to follow the marker arrows for the North Downs Way through the mixed woodland of Great Wood that includes oak, beech and some fine old yews. Watch for woodland sculpture on the left and magnificent views towards the

Sculpture in Great Wood

PUBLIC TRANSPORT Buses from Bluewater Shopping Centre and Gravesend. Enquiry line: 0870 6082608

REFRESHMENTS Snack café at country park or pubs with gardens in Trottiscliffe

PUBLIC TOILETS At the country park

ORDNANCE SURVEY MAP Explorer 148 (Maidstone & the Medway Towns)

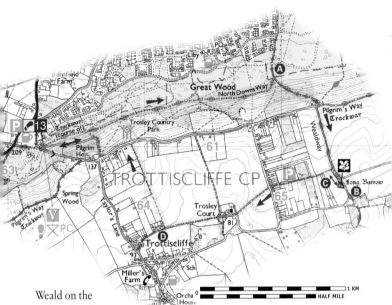

Weald on the
right. After about
¾ of a mile (1km) the path rises to
a kissing gate by a metal track gate
and leaves the country park.

Ⓐ Stay on the North Downs Way
as it turns right to descend the
slope of the Down via a sunken
lane. When the North Downs Way
meets the Pilgrim's Way turn right
for a few yards then left to pick up
the Weald Way as it runs along the
edge of a field on its journey south
through farmland. After about
500 yds (460m) ignore the
footpath signed to the right (pick
this up after visiting Coldrum Long
Barrow) and carry on along the
Weald Way to a cement track that
leads to the long barrow.

The remains of the Long Barrow

Ⓑ The barrow is atmospheric,
peaceful and an ideal spot to rest.
The path loops around it, via two

? *How many people
were buried in the
long barrow?*

St Peter and St Paul Church was a stopping point for pilgrims walking to Canterbury Cathedral along the nearby **Pilgrim's Way**. It has one bell, inscribed with the words 'William Hatch made me 1639'.

stiles, and there is an information panel at the bottom of its eastern slope.

C Rejoin the route by retracing the path northwards to turn left, leaving the Weald Way. The path crosses a field to a gate then runs between paddocks and gardens before entering a small car park. Leave the car park on an asphalt lane that meets a minor road. Cross this to enter a field and descend gently towards the church tower at Trosley Court. Turn right when the path meets an asphalt track leading to St Peter and St Paul Church. Take the bridleway between the buildings of Trosley Court, despite the private sign on the gate, then head westwards with a hedgerow on the left and farmland on the right.

D Turn right to skirt the gardens of houses and head back towards the downs. The well-marked path cuts across fields to climb gently to the Pilgrim's Way. Turn left to follow the Pilgrim's Way then turn right into the woodland just as it meets Taylor's Lane. The steep earth path rises to where steps make the climb slightly easier. At the top of these steps take the middle of three paths that leads upwards to rejoin the North Downs Way. Turn left along it to return to the car park. ●

St Peter and St Paul Church, Trosley

Alkham and Fidge's Wood

14

START Car park by Alkham village green

DISTANCE 4 miles

TIME 3 hours

PARKING Free by village green

ROUTE FEATURES Field paths and woodland tracks, some steep hills on the outward leg Children's play area by cricket field

This route climbs steeply out of the scenic Alkham valley to tackle the ups and downs of dry valleys and mixed woodland of the chalk downland before returning to the ancient village of Alkham.

From the car park walk towards the crossroads and cross the busy road to take Slip Lane. Turn left onto the footpath opposite a house called Evergreen. Walk through the churchyard of St Anthony's Church, passing the porch to leave by a kissing gate beneath a yew tree. The path passes a stone bench and then takes a stile into a field. Leave this field by a stile next to a large metal barn and then climb the steep hill to the top, crossing a series of stiles in hedges.

A Cross the byway into another field. Aim for the radio mast on the horizon and take the path by Colfir Farm to an asphalt lane. Turn right here along the lane to a T-junction by the house called Foxgloves. Take the stile at the junction and cross the field to a stile in the hedge 75 yds (69m) to the right of the metal gate in the corner of the field. Cross a small paddock to a stile and cross the driveway of Ellinge House into a small field. Veer diagonally right to the stile in the trees at the corner of the field and cross the driveway of Ellinge Cottage into a field sloping steeply down to a wood. Aim for the stile 75 yds (69m) to the left of the metal gate.

PUBLIC TRANSPORT Buses from Folkestone and Dover. Enquiry line: 0870 6082608

REFRESHMENTS Marquis of Granby, restaurant and outside tables

PUBLIC TOILETS None

ORDNANCE SURVEY MAP Explorer 138 (Dover, Folkestone & Hythe)

Alkham Bourne, which flows along the ditch by the village green, used to be known as Woe Waters because of the problems it has caused in the village. It is fed by an underground spring that rises when the water table reaches a certain level. In the floods of autumn and winter 2000–2001 the green was turned into a lake for months.

B Turn right along the asphalt lane and follow it until it turns sharply left by a byway. Take the byway, following bridleway signs, through the gate. Fidge's Wood is up the slope to the right. Watch for a gate on the right into the wood. Take the bridleway going left from the gate as it climbs through the mixed woodland to a gate into a field. Follow the line of trees until it stops then carry on straight ahead to a gate into a field. Carry on in the same direction, with Chalksole Green Farm in the

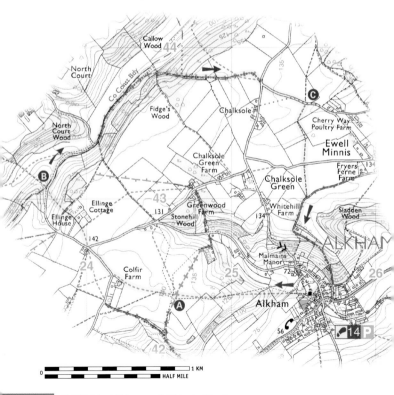

St Anthony's Church, Alkham

distance to the right, to leave the field at an asphalt lane. Turn right on the lane then immediately left in the direction of Ewell Minnis. After 300 yds (276m) watch for the footpath on the right where the lane curves to the left.

C Cross the stile into a field and head towards another stile by a metal gate. Cross into the next field and stay by its edge to another stile. From here veer right to follow the line of telegraph poles to a gap in the hedge. Cross the asphalt lane and over the next field towards the gap in the hedge in the corner. Turn right along a byway and follow as it descends past Pear Tree house, ignoring a path to the right. The path narrows and descends to the Alkham valley, crossing a field to a gate in the

trees. Take the asphalt lane and drop to the main road to turn right to the crossroads in Alkham by the children's play area. ●

? *Look at the walls of the house opposite the play area. Can you see its name?*

Wooded slopes near Alkham

15 Chartwell and Westerham

START Chartwell
DISTANCE 4½ miles
Time 3½ hours
PARKING Free at Chartwell visitors' car park
ROUTE FEATURES Some steep slopes on woodland paths and bridleways

This route starts at Chartwell, the former home of Sir Winston Churchill, and explores woods on its way to and from Westerham, birthplace of General James Wolfe. Although Chartwell is closed outside the March to November period, the visitors' car park and shop remain open.

Leave the estate by the entrance road for traffic and turn immediately right to take a footpath at a stile signed for the Greensand Way. Climb steeply between fences into the trees for 400 yds (368m) to an asphalt lane.

A Do not cross the lane but turn immediately left, leaving the Greensand Way, to descend through the woodland to the road. Do not cross the road.

B Take the footpath immediately on the right to re-enter the wood and climb Horn's Hill. At the top of the hill ignore a path crossing left to right and go straight ahead. Turn right at the next path crossroads then, after 100 yds

General James Wolfe, who died at the moment of his decisive victory over the French in 1759, went to school in **Westerham** and lived at Quebec House from 1727 to 1738. He joined the army at the age of 14 and was a major general at 32. His greatest military achievement, the storming of Quebec, cost him his life but secured Canada for the fledgling British Empire.

PUBLIC TRANSPORT Buses from Sevenoaks. Enquiry line: 0870 6082608. Trains from London and Hastings to Sevenoaks. Enquiry line: 0845 7484950
REFRESHMENTS Restaurant at Chartwell
PUBLIC TOILETS At Chartwell
ORDNANCE SURVEY MAP Explorer 147 (Sevenoaks & Tonbridge, Royal Tunbridge Wells & Westerham)

(92m), turn left at another crossroads to the road. Cross the road and take the path from the end of the layby.

C Do not go through the five-bar gate. Descend into Tower Wood, ignoring paths to left and right, to cross a wooden walkway crossing a boggy area then turn right, passing a garden. Turn right by the ornamental waterfall and leave the wood at a stile.

General James Wolfe is a celebrated son of Westerham

D Turn right and head to the top of the hill from where the church of St Mary the Virgin, in Westerham, can be seen. Descend the next field by the edge, skirting woodland planted to commemorate 100 years of Westerham parish council, to the gap by the holly in the corner. Cross a footbridge and stile to Mill Street which meets the A25 opposite Quebec House, the 17th century childhood home of General Wolfe.

Turn left here and enter the bustling heart of Westerham, watching for statues of both Wolfe and Churchill on the green. Turn left by the green, up the steps, following the sign for the Greensand Way along Water Lane, crossing a stream by a delightful bridge. Turn right after the kissing gate to another gate by a bridge and turn left to follow the Greensand Way. Take the right-hand stile by a house to climb between fences towards some trees.

M25

Court Lodge Sch

Green Croft

B 2024

P

0   1 KM
HALF MILE

A 25

Quebec House

109

Dunsdale

Farley Common

54

FBs   FB

Dunsdale Wood

Covers Farmhouse

MP

Westerham

Glebe House

173

Lodges Wood

142

Squerryes Court

Greensand Way

D

Hosey Hill

WESTERHAM CP

E

Squerryes Park

53

Hosey Common

158

Tower Wood

Twr

B 2026

44

53

45

C

194

French Street

Goodley Stock

fort

Horns Hill

B

A

d Way

Chart

Kent Hatch

Crockham House

52

P

P

15

Woodlands

189

Crockhamhill Common

Hosey Common Road

Chartwell

202

216

F

Mariners Hill

203

Meml

Chartwell Farm

Mapleton Road

Gudge Wood

124

Crockham Hill Farm

Froghole

51

B 2026

Crockham Hill

144

Ash

West House

Way

Sch

PO

Pootings

MP

Coachmans

Approaching Westerham form the south

E After the trees, leave the Greensand Way where it enters a wood and turn along the track to the top of the hill. On the other side of the hill, ignore the path to the left and carry on along the edge of the wood to bear left across the field towards Crockham House. Cross the stile and turn left, passing Crockham House to join a track through the wood. Remain on this bridleway, ignoring a footpath off the left, to rejoin the Greensand Way and pass the entrance to April Cottage.

> Winston Churchill lived at **Chartwell** from 1924 until his death in 1965. The house has many displays of his personal possessions and offers a fascinating insight into his life.

F Cross the road by Windmill Bank Cottage to take the left of two paths. At the top of the hill turn left and follow signs for Greensand Way, ignoring paths to left and right, to descend through the woods to the road opposite the entrance to Chartwell. ●

> *In what year was Westerham parish council formed?*

16 Chiddingstone and Weald woodland

START Castle Inn, Chiddingstone

DISTANCE 4.5 miles

TIME 3½ hours

PARKING Free on village street opposite primary school

ROUTE FEATURES Paths and tracks over undulating farmland and woodland.

This route is based around the countryside south of the ancient village of Chiddingstone with some careful route-finding necessary through Puckden and Yewtree woods. There is an alternative return route from Hill Hoath if families with young children wish to avoid the last 500 yds (460m) on the road.

Head eastwards from the Castle Inn, passing the Old Post Office and the 16th and 17th century houses facing the Church of St Mary the Virgin. To see the Chiding Stone turn right for a detour by a wooden millennium seat after the school. This route follows a footpath signed a few yards beyond the seat.

A Leave the road to take the path to the corner of the sports field and take the stile on the right. Cross a field, descending gently to skirt a copse then cross a stile into trees.

Millennium seat, Chiddingstone

Ignore the right-hand path, it leads to Hill Hoath and can be used as a return option. The path on the left veers away from the fence by mature oaks to meet the Eden Valley Walk. Turn left along the

PUBLIC TRANSPORT Buses from Edenbridge. Enquiry line: 0870 6082608. Trains from Tonbridge to Edenbridge. Enquiry line: 0845 7484950

REFRESHMENTS Castle Inn, Chiddingstone, has outside tables; Old Post Office tearoom and restaurant

PUBLIC TOILETS None

ORDNANCE SURVEY MAP Explorer 147 (Sevenoaks & Tonbridge, Royal Tunbridge Wells & Westerham)

Eden Valley Walk to a kissing gate. Enter woodland, the Slips, and leave via a stile onto a road.

B Turn right along the road for 30 yds (28m) to the path on the left leading to a gate into a paddock. Cross this diagonally to the opposite side to turn left along a track. After 300 yds (276m) leave the Eden Valley Walk by turning right along a bridleway at Watt Stock Farm. Follow the easy track that gently descends past Abbotsmerry Barn to join an asphalt drive leading past the pond and Salmans Oasts.

C Turn right through the kissing gate in front of Salmans House then left to climb wooden steps into a field. Stay by the edge of the field and leave by a kissing gate. Pass through the trees and cross a paddock by stiles into a field. Take the edge of the field by the trees to enter Russell's Wood. After a few yards, turn right to a stile and field. Take the path through the trees, passing ponds to climb gently to a stile leading to the driveway of Skipreed house. Go along the drive, watching for the stepped path to a stile on the right, opposite the next house, Oakenden Farm.

D Climb to the stile and turn right along the hedge, passing behind Skipreed to cross a new fence in the corner of the field. Descend to the wood and turn right after 10 yds (9m). The path eventually curves left and descends to a shallow gully then rises to a clearing. Go straight ahead, to the left of a metal gate, and skirt a sheep enclosure to a stile onto a track. Take the track to the road and turn right for 20 yds (18m) then pick up the path on the left opposite the house.

The Chiding Stone

E Follow the edge of the field and descend to the corner to cross a stream into Sliders wood. Just after the stream, take the right-hand path at the fork and follow it past a pond. Do not leave the wood by the first gate you come to but by the gate to the left of it. Follow the trees then pick up a track, passing a pond, to Hill Hoath Farm.

F *Those wanting to avoid the road section at the end can turn right along the Eden Valley*

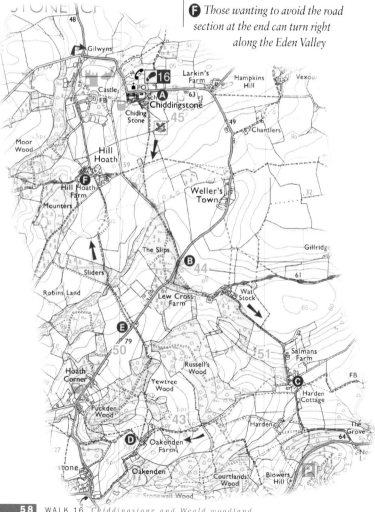

Walk here for 300 yds (276m), cross a track and take the path on the left, leaving the Eden Valley walk, to the copse on the outward leg. To return to Chiddingstone on the road pass through the farm and turn right on the asphalt track, eventually passing the entrance to Chiddingstone Castle. Turn right at the road junction to cross the ornamental castle lake to return to the village. ●

Oast-houses at Salmans Farm

How did the Chiding Stone get its name?

Oakenden Farm

17 Wye Downs and Crundale

This route starts at the Wye National Nature Reserve and follows a section of the North Downs Way, affording excellent views. After crossing farmland, the path climbs quickly to the church at Crundale and follows Crundale Downs, passing through woods to return.

START Car park above Broad Downs

DISTANCE 5 miles Time 4 hours

PARKING Free car park above Broad Downs

ROUTE FEATURES Paths and tracks across farmland and through woods. Fine views of Kent farmland.

Enter the gate to the Wye National Nature Reserve opposite the car park above Broad Downs. This reserve is home to many species of plants, including cowslips, rock roses and species of orchids, and animals, such as deer, rabbits and foxes.

Follow the path right, the North Downs Way, running parallel with the road. Ignore the gate to the Devil's Kneading Trough restaurant, but walk through the gate with English Nature written on it. Walk past the signpost marked with a yellow butterfly, ignoring the gate to the right. Follow this path and turn right until the road is reached.

A Cross the road and take the bridleway to the left. Follow the

The **Wye National Nature Reserve** is one of more than 200 reserves established to protect the most important areas of wildlife habitat and geological formations in Britain. Controlled grazing by sheep in the reserve encourages wild flowers and butterflies and it is the home to 19 species of orchid.

PUBLIC TRANSPORT Trains from Ashford and Canterbury to Wye. Enquiry line: 0845 7484950. Buses from Ashford to Wye. Enquiry line: 0870 6082608

REFRESHMENTS The Devil's Kneading Trough restaurant is open daily from 10.30am–5.30pm. Tables outside

PUBLIC TOILETS Wye

ORDNANCE SURVEY MAP Explorer 137 (Ashford, Headcorn, Chilham & Wye)

Easy walking near Crundale

edge of the fence. Extensive views over the village of Wye and the surrounding countryside can be seen from here. Walk to the end of the fence. The Wye Crown, a memorial carved in the hillside, is a short diversion of 200 yds (184m) farther along the North Downs Way. To continue to Crundale, take the gate at the end of the fence. Follow this path around the edge of the field and leave by a gate in the corner. Turn left on the track to go immediately through a second gate.

B On reaching the asphalt lane, turn right onto the track to eventually cross a stile onto a byway. Turn left along the track where hawthorn and ivy grow in profusion.

C Just before a clearing dominated by a mature tree, turn right into a large field. Do not take paths into Warren Wood. Follow the path diagonally across the field, looking carefully for the stile leading into a strip wood. Leave the wood, following the path diagonally

Chalk grassland on Crundale Downs

across the field. The path leaves a field in its corner. Go through a gate and turn immediately right to cross a stile. Walk up the grassy hill to a stile for a well-earned rest on the seats by the car park at the church of St Mary the Blessed Virgin. The church was damaged in the 1987 hurricane.

D Return to the stile you took to enter the church car park. Do not take the stile, but walk with the church on the left along Crundale Downs. As the path descends through woods evidence of coppicing can be seen. Turn right onto a track, passing many old yew trees. After 200 yds (184m), take the path sharply left

E Follow this path and go through the farm gates at the end.

The **Wye Crown** was carved in the chalk hillside in 1902 by students of Wye College to commemorate the coronation of Edward VII. Every year on Guy Fawkes' Night the students hold a torchlit procession from Wye to the memorial where they place the torches around the outline of the Crown.

Turn right to reach an asphalt lane near the entrance to Coombe Manor. Turn left here to come out on the road above the Wye National Nature Reserve. The car park is to the left after the Devil's Kneading Trough restaurant.   ●

? *At the entrance to the graveyard of the church there are some steps. What was their purpose?*

Chalk grassland at Wye Downs

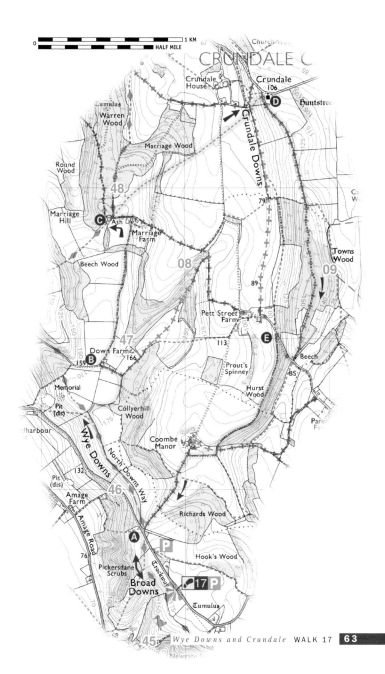

18 Sandwich and Sandwich Bay

This route starts at the historic former port of Sandwich and follows paths across drained farmland to the wide, pebble beach at Sandwich Bay before returning across a golf course.

START The Quay, Sandwich
DISTANCE 5.5 miles
TIME 4 hours
PARKING Pay and display at the Quay
ROUTE FEATURES Flat and well-marked paths Children's play area In park near Quay

Leave the car park with the River Stour on the left, passing the slipway and the beacon. Pass the double gates into parkland and head for a children's play area.

A Turn right, following signs for the Saxon Shore Way. Pass the tennis club, turn right at the road to cross the bridge then turn left along the line of the old town wall. Ignore the path going left down steps but follow the curve of the old wall, passing allotments and bowling greens. At New Street, leave the Saxon Shore Way and turn left to cross the railway line, passing St Bartholemew's Chapel.

The River Stour at Sandwich

PUBLIC TRANSPORT Trains from Dover and Canterbury. Enquiry line: 0845 7484950. Buses from Canterbury and Ramsgate. Enquiry line: 0870 6082608
REFRESHMENTS Pubs, cafés and restaurants in Sandwich
PUBLIC TOILETS The Quay car park
ORDNANCE SURVEY MAP Explorer 150 (Canterbury & the Isle of Thanet)

B Where the main road bends to the right take the footpath on the left along the asphalt path. Follow it as it veers left away from the drainage dyke. Eventually, cross the dyke by the footbridge and turn left by the white house onto a bridleway along the asphalt track. The track curves right towards Temptye Farmhouse. Over to the right is the spire of the church in Worth village. Turn left at the farmhouse, taking the track past Little Temptye. Carry on straight ahead at Blue Pigeons Farm, ignoring the bridleway to the right, to cross the railway line.

Every year on August 25 at **St Bartholemew's Chapel**, Sandwich, local children do a 'bun run' around the building which symbolises the journeying of ancient travellers. The bun represents the meal offered by townsfolk to travellers.

C Follow the path to Little Downs Bridge across North Stream, passing by the curve of the stream to pick up a track by a second curve in the river. Follow the track, ignoring a footpath to left and right, to pass the Sandwich Bay Bird Observatory to Guilford Road.

Easy walking over drained farmland

D Go straight across the road to the stile into the field and cross to the corner. Follow cement footpath markers to enter the golf course. Follow the mown path across the course, watching for more cement footpath markers. Leave the golf course, cross Princes Drive to the beach. This is Sandwich Bay. To the north is Pegwell Bay, where St Augustine landed to bring Christianity to England in 597. The Saxons also landed here. The town beyond is Ramsgate.

E Turn left along the shore. The best walking is between the beach and the road, on the grassy path. Turn left by the public toilet block to take the stile back onto

North Stream near Sandwich

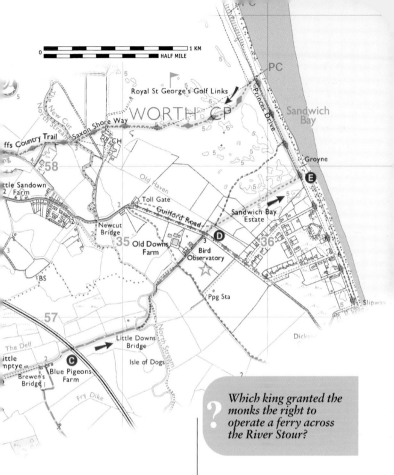

the golf course. Follow the well-
marked paths across a fairway, past
the clubhouse to a kissing gate.
Cross an asphalt track to a stile
leading to a footbridge. Pick up the
asphalt path, ignoring an asphalt
path to the right, cross a footbridge
and turn right to return to the path
by the children's playpark and the
outward route.   ●

Pebble beach at Sandwich Bay

19 *Five Oak Green and Golden Green*

This flat route follows a figure of eight from Five Oak Green to Golden Green, crossing the River Medway at East Lock, a particularly attractive spot. The smaller River Bourne forms the northern boundary of the walk. The path returns through fields and orchards banded by streams and drainage ditches.

START Post office, Five Oak Green

DISTANCE 5½ miles

TIME 4 hours

PARKING Free at recreation ground, Five Oak Green

ROUTE FEATURES Well-marked paths across fields and orchards crossing two rivers

Start at the post office in Five Oak Green, cross the road and turn right into Whetsted Road. Cross the bridge over the railway line and turn immediately left.

A Walk through the pear and apple orchards to the footbridge just before Moat Farm. Follow the yellow arrows around the farm buildings to cross another footbridge to a track running to the left of the main drainage ditch. Cross two concrete footbridges.

Concrete **pillboxes** were part of the defences that were hastily erected in 1940 in preparation for the expected German invasion of Britain in the Second World War. They were built at strategic points, such as road junctions and the crossing points of rivers and canals.

B Take the path straight ahead towards East Lock, ignoring the path on the right. East Lock, on the River Medway, is an attractive site for a picnic. Cross the bridges and follow the path between the two

PUBLIC TRANSPORT Buses from Tonbridge and Paddock Wood. Enquiry line: 0870 6082608. Trains from Tonbridge and Ashford to Paddock Wood. Enquiry line: 0845 7484950

REFRESHMENTS Beer gardens at Queens Head and Kings Head, Five Oak Green. Bell Inn, Golden Green, has tables outside.

PUBLIC TOILETS Recreation ground, Five Oak Green

ORDNANCE SURVEY MAP Explorer 136 (The Weald, Royal Tunbridge Wells, Cranbrook, Hawkhurst & Bewl Water)

pillboxes towards the houses of Golden Green, ignoring the path going left.

C Turn left along the road at Golden Green then right into Victoria Road just before the Bell Inn. Cross the River Bourne and turn right onto the path running alongside it. Recross the river at a footbridge, ignoring the path on the right, to join the Wealdway.

The River Medway at Ford Green Bridge

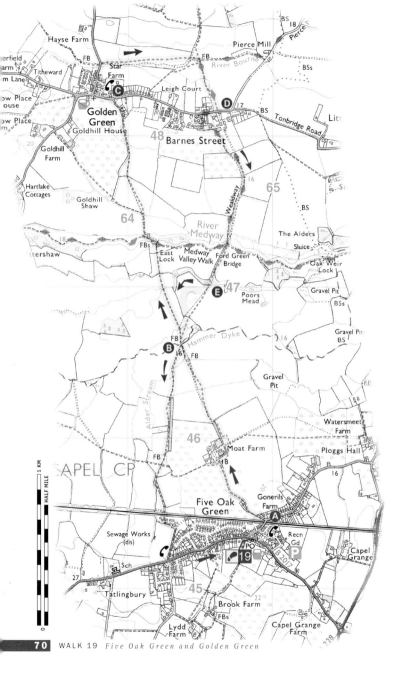

Oast-houses near Barnes Street

After 200 yds (184m) do not take the gate but bear slightly left to reach the road in Barnes Street.

D Turn right onto the road for 50 yds (46m) then turn left onto the path to follow marker posts through some farm buildings. The route now follows a clear stream then recrosses the River Medway

Footbridge over Hammer Dyke

at Ford Green Bridge. Take the stile onto the path along the edge of the wood and after 200 yds (184m) enter the trees to reach a stile.

E Leave the trees and skirt the fence around the lake to cross a field to the concrete footbridge crossed on the outward leg. Take the right-hand path past the hanging vines and under the railway. From here, the track leads to the main road at Five Oak Green. Turn left to return to the start of the walk and the car park. ●

> **?** *Which national trail does the path follow for some of its route?*

20 Cobham and Henley Down

START Village hall, Cobham

DISTANCE 5½ miles

TIME 4 hours

PARKING Free at Cobham village hall, known as the Meadow Room

ROUTE FEATURES Gentle paths through fields and orchards with one steep section to reach the crest of Henley Down.

This walk starts in Cobham, which has many associations with Charles Dickens. The historic village also has an ancient church and haunted pub with secret tunnels. The route then heads south to organic farmland at the top of Henley Down, follows the chalk ridge of the Downs and returns through apple and pear orchards.

Turn left out of the entrance to the village hall car park towards the village centre, passing the village pump.

Almost opposite the Leather Bottle, turn right to take the steps into the churchyard of St Mary Magdalene. Take the path by the church tower to an asphalt lane leading to a smaller graveyard. Leave the graveyard by the stile in the corner, heading south along the edge of a field. Views open up to the east as the path passes under power lines to leave the field

through a gap in the trees. Turn left along the asphalt lane to the bridge across the railway line.

A After crossing the bridge, leave the road by taking the path on the right into the field before Batts Cottages. Continue to the corner of the field where the path enters a short tunnel of undergrowth to a kissing gate and a small paddock.

> **?** *What is the name of the rock used in the walls by the village water pump?*

PUBLIC TRANSPORT Buses from Gravesend and Rochester. Enquiries: 0870 6082608. Trains from Rochester to Sole Street. Enquiry line: 0845 7484950

REFRESHMENTS Pubs with outside tables and gardens in Cobham

PUBLIC TOILETS The sports pavilion, Cobham recreation ground

ORDNANCE SURVEY MAP Explorer 148 (Maidstone & the Medway Towns); Explorer 163 (Gravesend & Rochester)

The Leather Bottle, Cobham

for 10 yds (9m) and take the stile on the right into the field. Walk uphill diagonally to the left, aiming for the stile where the wooden fence meets the trees. Walk upwards through the trees to a kissing gate leading into a field. Head in a south-easterly direction, taking a diagonal line across the field where the path gently rises. Leave the field by a stepped path through trees to reveal superb views from the crest of the Down. Below lies the hamlet of Luddesdown.

Cross this to another gate where there are now views across to Henley Down and Henley Wood. Descend the field to Henley Street, where the path takes a narrow cut between fences to a road. Turn left

B The land around here is farmed organically. This is evident in the summer months when the wheat fields are strewn with poppies. Turn right along the crest of the Down, crossing a stile to pick up the Wealdway. After about

Houses by St Mary Magdalene churchyard, Cobham

100 yds (92m) turn right at a fence corner to stay on the Wealdway on a stepped path to a stile. Follow the edge of the field to a dogwalkers' stile that leads into trees. Keep to the edge of a U-shaped clearing, with the trees close on the right and a pylon on the left. Descend gently towards an opening in the trees where marker posts signed for the Wealdway indicate the route ahead. Ignore routes to left and right until a lone house on the left is passed then a pond on the right. Ignore the bridleway going to the right but look for the path junction just past it, where the route leaves the Wealdway.

C Turn right to take the right-hand path in the direction of Cobham which can be seen in the distance. This well-marked path crosses farm fields to the footbridge over the railway line. Enter an orchard and head diagonally to the right (in the direction of two pylons) to a gap in a hedge leading onto an asphalt lane. Cross this to the kissing gate leading into a pear orchard. Do not turn right towards the corner of the field but walk straight ahead for a few yards between the lines of trees to where the path can be seen cutting through the lines of fruit trees. Go through the boundary hedge and head up a grassy strip towards a lone oak. Careful route-

Organic farmland on Henley Down

finding is needed until the path becomes apparent. Note that some of the support poles for the trees are marked with yellow paint, confounding those who are looking for a yellow footpath marker. Pass to the right of the oak to take the grassy strip separating older fruit trees from younger ones. At the end of a boundary hedge look for the obvious line of the path cutting through the trees. Eventually, the mature trees by the Church of St Mary

Charles Dickens used to walk in the grounds of Cobham Hall with his friend the Earl of Darnley. He also visited the Leather Bottle Inn, immortalising it in the *Pickwick Papers*.

Magdalene come into view. Enter the graveyard through a metal kissing gate and turn left up the lane back towards the church. ●

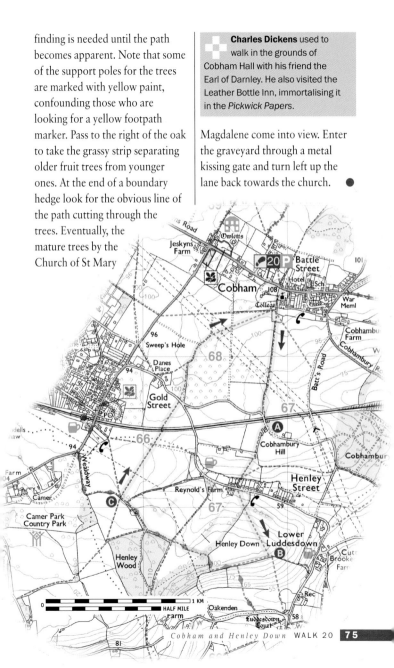

Further Information

Always take with you both warm and waterproof clothing and sufficient food and drink. Wear suitable footwear, i.e. strong walking boots or shoes that give a good grip over stony ground, on slippery slopes and in muddy conditions. Try to obtain a local weather forecast and bear it in mind before you start. Do not be afraid to abandon your proposed route and return to your starting point in the event of a sudden and unexpected deterioration in the weather.

All the walks described in this book will be safe to do, given due care and respect, even during the winter. Indeed, a crisp, fine winter day often provides perfect walking conditions, with firm ground underfoot and a clarity of light unique to that time of the year.

The most difficult hazard likely to be encountered is mud, especially when walking along woodland and field paths, farm tracks and bridleways – the latter in particular can often get churned up by cyclists and horses. In summer, an additional difficulty may be narrow and overgrown paths, particularly along the edges of cultivated fields. Neither should constitute a major problem provided that the appropriate footwear is worn.

Leeds is one of England's loveliest castles

Follow the Country Code

- Enjoy the countryside and respect its life and work
- Guard against all risk of fire
- Take your litter home
- Fasten all gates
- Help to keep all water clean
- Keep your dogs under control
- Protect wildlife, plants and trees
- Keep to public paths across farmland
- Take special care on country roads
- Leave livestock, crops and machinery alone

The view across fields to Chillenden Mill

- Make no unnecessary noise
- Use gates and stiles to cross fences, hedges and walls

(The Countryside Agency)

Useful Organisations

Council for the Protection of Rural England
128 Southwark St,
London SE1 0SW
Tel: 0207 981 2800

Countryside Agency
John Dower House, Crescent Place, Cheltenham GL50 3RA.
Tel. 01242 521381

English Heritage
23 Savile Row, London W1X 1AB.
Tel. 0171 973 3250; Fax 0171 973 3146; Website www.english-heritage.org.uk
South West Regional Office
Tel. 0845 3010 007

English Nature
Northminster House,
Peterborough PE1 1UA.
Tel. 01733 455100; Fax 01733 455103; E-mail enquiries@english-nature.org.uk; Website www.english-nature.org.uk

National Trust
Membership and general enquiries:
PO Box 39, Bromley, Kent BR1 3XL.
Tel. 0181 315 1111; E-mail

enquires@ntrust.org.uk; Website
www.nationaltrust.org.uk
South East Regional Office
Tel. O1372 453401

Ordnance Survey
Romsey Road, Maybush,
Southampton SO16 4GU.
Tel. 08456 05 05 05 (Lo-call)

Ramblers' Association
2nd Floor, Camelford House,
87–90 Albert Embankment,
London SE1 7TW.
Tel. 020 7339 8500

Youth Hostels Association
(Head Office) Trevelyan House,

Dimple Road, Matlock,
Derbyshire DE4 3YH
Tel. 01629 592600 (General
enquiries)
Website: www.yha.org.uk

*Local Organisations and Places
of Interest*
For prices and opening hours for
places of interest visited during the
walks in this book:

Chiddingstone Castle
Tel. 01892 870347
Sissinghurst Castle
Tel. 01580 710700
Leeds Castle
Tel. 01622 765400

Crossing fields near the River Medway